The WHISPERS of MY WOES

KAE WATSON

PAGE PUBLISHING
Conneaut Lake, PA

First originally published by Page Publishing 2024

ISBN 979-8-89315-428-3 (pbk)
ISBN 979-8-89315-441-2 (digital)

Printed in the United States of America

PREFACE

In the quiet corners of our mind, where shadows dance and dreams take flight, lies a realm where the whispers of our deepest woes blend with the melodies of our journey through life. It is within this ethereal space that the essence of this collection, *The Whispers of My Woes*, finds its resonance.

In the delicate dance of words and emotions that became *The Whispers of My Woes*, I find myself compelled to express my deepest gratitude to the unwavering pillars of my existence—my family.

To my mommy and her mommy (Mommom), whose love and encouragement have been the foundation on which my dreams could flourish, thank you for instilling in me the courage to pen down the echoes of my soul. The pillar of your support and belief in my creative journey has been my guiding light.

To my sisters, Ashleigh, Tierra, and Jae, who have been my partners in both laughter and solace in times of tears, your presence has filled the pages of my life with vibrant hues. Your understanding and camaraderie have been my inspiration to explore the intricacies of our emotions through poetry.

To my family, close friends, and all those who have been a part of this literary expedition, your encouragement and belief in my abilities have fueled my determination to share my whispered woes with the world.

In this symphony of life, my family has been the melody that harmonizes with every word, creating a composition that reflects the essence of who I am. This book is not just mine; it is ours—a collective endeavor of love, support, and shared experiences.

With heartfelt gratitude, Kae.

Whispers on a Tear-Stained Paper

Beneath the veil of moonlit night,
I bear a burden hidden from sight
No soul on earth can truly see
The depths of who I strive to be
But in quiet's soft embrace
With this pen in hand, I find my grace
These tearstained pages, my confidant
Where secrets flow without a haunt
No judgment here, just ink and rhyme
A sanctuary transcending time
I pour my heart, my soul, my pain
On paper canvas there is no disdain
For here, I am truly free
To share my truths, my mystery
No eyes to watch, no whispers near
Just this pen and paper to hold dear
With every stroke my spirit is bared
My hidden self no longer snared
In the silence, I become whole

A story told a wounded soul
So let this pen and tearstained sheet
Be my escape, my solace, my heartbeat
No one may know the real me,
But in these lines, I am set free.

JOURNAL ENTRY

DANCES WITH LIFE

In this intricate weaving of my life, woven with threads of hope and ambition, there exists a darker hue that stains the fabric—a color born of failure, a relentless shadow that clings to my every step. It's a presence that obscures the path ahead, leaving me stranded in the desolate landscape of my own inadequacies.

As I traverse this barren terrain, the weight of my shortcomings becomes an oppressive burden, each misstep etching a painful narrative onto the canvas of my soul. The echoes of my failures reverberate like a dissonant symphony, drowning out the delicate melodies of triumph that once played in the recesses of my mind.

The relentless cadence of my own disappointment becomes a haunting refrain, an unbearable sound that pierces the silence of my contemplations. It is a sound that reverberates through the corridors of my consciousness, a constant reminder of promises unkept and dreams unrealized.

The pain of letting others down, like a searing brand upon my heart, leaves an indelible mark that refuses to fade. Faces once filled with trust now reflect the disappointment I've sown, and in their eyes, I glimpse the wreckage of shattered expectations. I am haunted by the knowledge that my actions, or lack thereof, have cast a shadow upon those who believed in me.

In the quiet moments of reflection, I find myself standing at the intersection of remorse and self-discovery. The road ahead is obscured by the fog of past mistakes, and I grapple with the fear that my failures may define the chapters yet to be written. Yet, in this crucible of introspection, there exists a glimmer of resilience—a determination to rise from the ashes of defeat.

For even in the darkest corners of my soul, I must find the strength to illuminate the path forward. The narrative of failure, though written in ink that seems indelible, is not the final chapter. I must learn to see beyond the stains on the tapestry and recognize the potential for growth that lies dormant within me.

As I confront the pain of letting others down, I understand that redemption is not found in erasing the past, but in forging a future marked by resilience and self-discovery. The symphony of failure may play on, but I am determined to compose a counterpoint of triumph—a melody that rises above the dissonance and charts a course toward redemption.

Sanctuary of Shadows

In the depths of my sanctuary, where shadows
dance their silent waltz,
My room, a haven, now crumbles 'neath the
weight of hidden faults.
Monsters, not of claw and fang, but burdens
heavy, unseen,
They gather 'round, a haunting choir, in dark-
ness, they convene.

Each night they come to tuck me in, beneath the
veil of sleep,
Their whispers soft, their touch a chill, their
presence mine to keep.
For in this chamber where I sought solace, they
found their domain,
And I, their master, in slumber's grasp, succumb
to their refrain.

Beneath the bed they hide away, the burdens I
    dare not face,
Their weight upon my weary soul, a never-end-
    ing chase.
They claw and gnaw at sanity, haunting every
    dream,
Their shadows cast upon my mind, an ever-grow-
    ing stream.

Yet still, I play the role of host, the keeper of this
    darkened lair,
For to confront these burdens head-on, seems a
    task too much to bear.
So, I surrender to their embrace, as nightfall
    softly creeps,
Becoming both the captor and the captive, in
    this realm where sorrow seeps.

But in the quiet hours before dawn, when dark-
    ness starts to wane,
I sense a glimmer of hope, a flicker in the pain.
For though the burdens linger on, and haunt me
    through the night,

I know that with the breaking dawn, I'll find the
    strength to fight.

So, let the monsters come and tuck me in as I lie
    still and weak,
For in this dance of shadows, I'll find the courage
    that I seek.
And when the morning light does come, I'll rise
    to face the day,
No longer bound by burdens, I'll cast the mon-
    sters away.

Anxiety's Poetic Tale

A victim of tragedies, I carry their weight,
Anxiety's grip tightens, sealing my fate,
Hopes for the future eclipsed by fear's reign,
Annexed in my mind, where torment is the chain.
Fear tucks me in, a sinister embrace,
Kissing me goodnight, as nightmares find their
    place,
They flourish and dance in the shadows of night,
A symphony of terror, a haunting flight.

Grim Reaper's specter, I dare to implore,
To end this agony, to close pain's door,
Yet anxiety's grip, it holds me so near,
A captive to its power, consumed by its sheer.
Tightness like a vice, the grip is profound,
Lost is my light, as darkness surrounds,
But deep within, a flicker remains,
A glimmer of hope, despite anxiety's chains.

In this struggle, my spirit yet fights,
To break free from the darkness, reclaim the
heights,
For even in agony, strength finds its way,
Through the darkest of nights, a resilient ray.

Untitled

I never wanted to give you any credit,
For my pain, your absence, I won't edit.
I never truly felt your love or care,
An abundance of love, I had to spare.
Not replacement love, just love in plenty,
I never needed yours, I was never empty.
But now a new phase of life's begun,
Issues plague me, tied to what you've done.
I don't seek reasons, why you weren't there,
I only blame you, this burden I bear.

Your love for me, it's a mystery,
Do you even love me? It's hard to see.
You don't even know me, not deep inside,
What could you love? The stories, they hide.
Unconditional, you say, but what's the truth?
Without conditions, it's like a mirage, aloof.

How do I accept love, when part is missing,
I'm half your creation, there's no dismissing.

So I place the blame on you, heavy and cold,
For my shortcomings, and the shame I hold.
I'll release them like doves, let them fly,
Lay them on your shoulders, let out a sigh.
A burden that weighs you down, for truth,
The least you can do, for the pain your absence
    put me through.

I hope these words cut deeper than anyone can
    see,
The sweetest karma for the hurt you caused to
    me.
After all, I am my mother's daughter, true,
And in her strength, I'll find my own
    breakthrough.
This is my poem, my words to convey,
The emotions I feel, in my own way.
Blame and burden, I cast them aside,
And in this new chapter, my old self has died.

Solitudes Grip

Alone within a room's quiet expanse,
A haunting feeling takes its stance,
Existence wanes when solitude nears,
A fading ember, engulfed by fears.
In isolation's grip, I start to fade,
A specter lost, in shadows displayed,
No heartbeats echo, no voices near,
A void unfilled, a soul gripped by sear.

Alone, I cease to share heart's space,
Those who matter, gone without a trace,
No calls, no messages to soothe the soul,
A hollow echo, an empty role.
Yet, in this stillness, a darkness blooms,
A thought that lingers, of impending dooms,
Should I yield to the abyss within,
Release all burdens, let despair begin?

But hark, a light within the gloom,
A voice that whispers, dispelling doom,

For in the darkness, strength may rise,
A chance to heal, to mend heart's ties.
Alone yet not forgotten, it's true,
A part of me remains in all I do,
The burden shared, a weight combined,
A tapestry of lives, forever aligned.

So let not darkness claim the day,
For within your heart, love finds its way,
In solitude, seek the strength to be,
A light that shines, resilient, and free.

Rain's Caress

Reflecting on pain, standing in rain's caress,
Each drop a memory, a bitter distress,
Piercing through like shards of the past,
Tears and fears mingling, a stormy contrast.
Coldness wraps around, numbing the core,
Yet within the chill, a cleansing downpour,
Tears blend with rain, a symphony's grace,
A fresh chapter emerges, a new life to embrace.
With rain's gentle touch, pain's grip releases,
A feeling of cleansing, as soul's turmoil ceases,
Washing away the shadows that once held true,
A canvas reborn, painted skies in a different hue.

Amidst the gloomy clouds, memories reside,
A testament to the storms, life can't hide,
But as birds take flight and sunlight starts to
    gleam,
A new day dawns, a chance to redeem.
God's masterpiece above, the canvas vast,
Sun breaking through, shadows don't last,

A new beginning unveiled in skies so wide,
A transformation unfurls, a rebirth inside.

So I sit and stare, a contemplative gaze,
At the rain-kissed world, where healing paves,
A path toward the future, where hope sets free,
A new self emerges, who I'm meant to be.

Bound by Time

Time is like a noose that society so gently slips,
Over my neck, I fear to kick the chair of expecta-
    tions, tight as whips.
Hung by my own failures, each breath a silent
    scream,
Dreams clawing from my lungs, lost in the
    unseen.

Love's Celestial Promise

To my loved ones, I vow to stand and fight,
In your embrace, I find my endless might.
But if fate should call me from this earthly sphere,
Know that my love for you will persevere.

I'll paint the skies with hues of purplish grace,
Replacing blue with twilight's warm embrace.
The moon shall glow, a beacon in the night,
A silver orb, a source of gentle light.

I'll scatter stars across the boundless sky,
A million eyes that never say goodbye.
Though I may part from this world we know,
My love will shine in every star's soft glow.
So when you gaze upon the heavens high,
Remember me, and let your spirits fly.
For in those celestial wonders, you'll find,
A love that lasts, an eternal bind.

Whispers of Grace

In the quiet moments of today,
I find solace in the beauty that surrounds,
A whisper of hope dances in the air,
Promising a better tomorrow,
Yet, amidst this delicate dance,
Lurks the shadow of tragedy,
For hope, it seems, is but faith in the unknown.

What if tomorrow never graces us with its light?
What if faith fails to deliver its promises?
Questions linger like shadows in the night,
And uncertainty casts its long, daunting shadow,
But in the midst of it all,
There lies a truth, a glimmer of light,
A reminder to cherish the beauty of today.

For today holds its own magic,
Its own imperfect perfection,
In every laugh, every tear,
Every fleeting moment,

There is beauty to be found,
And in embracing its flaws,
We find a kind of grace,
A quiet acceptance of the now.

So I'll linger here, in the beauty of today,
Never taking its imperfections for granted,
For even amidst the uncertainty,
There is a certain peace,
A reminder that in this moment, I am alive,
And that in itself, is a gift worth treasuring.

Flaws as a Masterpiece

In the garden of our beings, a symphony of selves,
Where perfection's gleaming towers, conceal their hollow shells.
We've been sold a flawless future, a life devoid of strife,
Yet in every perfect picture, something's missing: real life.

Up, up the winding stairways, endless peak in sight,
Round and round, we lose ourselves, in the pursuit of right.
Grasping for golden trophies, in the mirage of accomplishment,
Yet the heart starves in silence, yearning for contentment.

Now, it's time to make space, for the cloudy days and rain,

For the beautiful and the broken, for pleasure
    and for pain.
To not just look at failure, with an impatient
    sigh,
But see in it, a comrade, a friend passing by.

Let's make space for the off-key notes, in our har-
    monious song,
For the moments we stumble, the times we get
    it wrong.
For the beauty in the failing, and strength within
    the scar,
The rhapsody in pieces, is who we truly are.

Imperfections are the seams, that stitch our sto-
    ries whole,
They carve our edges, mold us, the masterpiece
    of soul.
Each and every blemish, is but a golden thread,
Weaving through our being, into a mosaic
    widespread.

It's not about erasing, it's not about the repair,

It's about embracing blemishes, as proof that we
    were there.
Our imperfections beckon, with a wisdom all
    their own,
Telling us how far we've come, and how much
    we've grown.

So let's make space for imperfections, let them in
    with grace,
For in the heart's veneer of cracks, the light finds
    its place.
And in that sacred, scattered light, we'll find our
    truest state,
Imperfect, but still resilient, and undeniably
    great.

JOURNAL ENTRY

2

SHADOWS OF GRIEF

Grief is a familiar companion, a constant presence that has intricately woven itself into the fabric of my existence. It is my shadow, the darkest one, that stretches across my soul when the light is cast upon me. Throughout my life, I have been intimately acquainted with death, a harsh lesson learned too early—a realization that life, no matter how vibrant, is not eternal. My loved ones attempted to rationalize the pain, offering explanations like "they died of old age, so be at peace" or "tragedy may hurt more, but our time is our time. Be grateful." Yet, for me, each departure inflicted an unfathomable pain. I struggled to reconcile with the cause or quantify the loss; all I knew was that someone who had been a part of my every breath, someone meant to achieve greatness alongside me, someone from whom I learned the true meaning of care, was no longer present. The burden of constant grieving weighed heavily on my shoulders, a relentless reminder that I would never see them again. Their absence echoed in the void of laughter, the unspoken "I love you," and the irreplaceable essence of who they were. To receive gut-wrenching news from a loved one about the departure of another added another layer of heartache. Knowing that they had taken their last breath left me grappling with the harsh reality that they were gone forever. Grief is as intricate and complex as life itself. The pain of knowing that I will never witness them draw breath again sometimes makes me question the fairness of my own existence over theirs. It becomes a profound struggle, a battle against the seemingly unjust nature of life. A profound lesson taught by grief is that the stages of mourning are not linear; they don't neatly conclude, allowing one to move on to the next. Shock, denial, anger, bargaining, depression, reconstruction, and acceptance become constant companions, accompanying me every day after a loss until the inevitable day when it becomes my turn. Yet, within the labyrinth of grief, I have discovered a hidden beauty. It lies in the immortalization of those I have lost. Their teachings, the memories forged, the love and laughter shared, and the poems penned in their honor have become timeless echoes of their essence and love. Within my relationship with grief, I have found a way to celebrate the enduring impact of those who have left, ensuring they remain eternally alive. Within me, they are immortalized.

Echoes of Grief/ Deion's Unforeseen Melody

No forewarning came of grief's cruel might,
Loved ones departed, leaving aching fright,
I bore farewells before, but this one, a sting,
A pain so deep, a sorrow that does cling.
Is it age, is it the maturing heart's ache,
That amplifies loss, as emotions break?

Your absence, a wound that refuses to mend,
A part of me lost, a heartache to transcend.
Once I felt you near, a presence so dear,
But now, a fog obscures what once was clear.
How am I to journey on, so incomplete,
Without the heartbeat of our shared heart's beat?
My heart's song was ours, a harmonious strain,
But now it's a solo, an echo of pain,
No longer two hearts that rhythmically blend,
Just my heartbeat left, a tune without end.

My life mirrors the soul's ache and despair,
Chasing distant goals, a path tenuous and rare,
But success remains elusive, just out of view,
For who I was, without you, it no longer holds
    true.

Yet strength is found in knowing you persist,
Existing in what's present, future, and missed,
Through the passage of time, your essence
    remains,
A constant, unchanging, in joys and in pains.

This journey through sorrow, a symphony
    untold,
In the cadence of tears, in the stories of old,
In echoes of grief, a melody unforeseen,
I find solace in the thought that you've never
    been.
For in every moment, and all that will be,
Your spirit resides, an eternal decree,
Though the notes may alter, the melody will go
    on,
A tribute to the love that forever lives on.

I Stand in Darkness, Looking for Your Light

I stand in the darkness, denying the truth,
Refusing the whispers that speak of your flight.
The shadows persist, as sadness takes root,
But I'll resist, warding off the fateful night.

I shield my heart from the pain and despair,
Tricking my mind into believing a lie.
In this web of denial, I find solace and care,
Burying grief, letting truth pass me by.

Yet, deep down I know this facade won't prevail,
For truth shines bright, piercing through the
    haze.
Denial crumbles, and truth's strength will prevail,
Peeling away the mask, in sorrow's blaze.

No more shall denial, be my soul's shelter,
I'll face the night, embracing the truth, set me
    free.

Tears of Fury

Oh, flames of fury, burning bright and free,
Engulfing my heart in anger's fierce caress.
In your scorching blaze, I find solace, you see,
A way to express the pains I cannot erase.
Your raging tempest consumes my every thought,
And I unleash my rage, a torrential storm.

Words of wrath cascade, with vengeance wrought,
And in this fiery dance, emotions transform.
But as the ashes settle and fury subsides,
I'm left with the wreckage of words spoken in
    haste.
Anger's grip, gentled by regret's tides,
I yearn for peace, a state to be embraced.
For anger, though cathartic, can't be my shield,
From grief's cruel grasp, a new path shall be
    revealed.

An Offering to Fate

I bargain with fate, plead my way through the
 night,
Offering my dreams, my hopes, my soul's desire,
In exchange for one more heartfelt goodbye.
Oh, fickle fate, I implore with tearful plea,
To rewind time, to undo what has transpired,
To grant me solace, to find peace again.

I yearn for a sign, a glimmer of reprise,
To bridge the chasm between heaven and earth,
To have a dialogue transcending time.
But bargaining proves futile, for what's done is
 done,
No negotiation can rewrite destiny's script.
I'll embrace the memories, cherish each rhyme,
For in acceptance, growth, and healing shall find
 grip.

Moonlit Villanelle: A Deal Within the Night

In the moonlit night, I made a bargain true,
Pleading with the stars, seeking solace unfurled.
A solemn vow, my deepest desires I'd pursue,
To have one more moment, unfettered by this
world.

Pleading with the stars, seeking solace unfurled,
I bargained with the night, with dreams as my
guide.
To have one more moment, unfettered by this
world,
Through silent whispers, my plea would reside.
I bargained with the night, with dreams as my
guide,
A sacred pact formed, while shadows danced
around.

Through silent whispers, my plea would reside,
Searching for solace, in the moonlit ground.
A sacred pact formed, while shadows danced
     around,
Yet deals in the moonlight, can't rewrite the stars.
Searching for solace, in the moonlit ground,
I embrace acceptance, healing my battle scars.

Deceptive Illusions

Deceptive Illusions,
Autumn leaves flutter,
Whispers of life, now absent,
Grief's veil shields truth.

A Hollow Melody

A hollow melody plays within my soul,
A mournful tune that echoes far and wide.
Grief's symphony, in somber tones, takes hold,
Leading me down a path where emotions collide.
Each note a reminder of a joy now departed,
A melancholic dance, embraced by despair.
But within this melody, healing is imparted,
A unique rhythm that helps me repair.

Though the void may seem vast, the pain
    consuming,
The melody whispers of solace and renewal.
Through each sorrowful note, a healing arises,
And within each refrain, hope's arrival.

Echoes of Evermore

The past unfolds its petals, a garden of yesterdays,
Every bloom a reminder, dissolving all fears.
I miss you, a whisper in the winds that softly sigh,
Yet, in every memory, you're a forever sky.

Your laughter, a melody, woven in time's embrace,
A symphony of moments, a dance in grace.
Though distance may part, and time may
        intervene,
You remain in the heart, in the spaces between.

So, here in the echoes, in the silence we share,
Your presence endures, a solace so rare.
For every memory, a beacon shining bright,
I wish you were here, in the softness of the night.

Echoes of Absence

In the depths of sorrow, I reside,
Life without you, so cruel, a relentless tide.
Unreal, it seems, this world without your grace,
Each dawn, your absence, I must face.
Every breath I take, a sigh of regret,
For without you, life is but a silhouette.
How can I breathe, knowing you're no more,
A soul departed to an unknown shore?

This sadness tempts me, to join your realm,
For if you can't live, why should I overwhelm?
It feels unjust, this burden I bear alone,
The guilt of breathing, a weight like a stone.
Each failure I encounter, a pain profound,
For it feels like I let you down.

But in this darkness, a flicker of hope I find,
To cherish this life, and not leave it behind.
For in the midst of despair, I see the way,

To honor your memory, and seize the day.
Though you're gone, I'll live with your love in
     sight,
In the darkness, I'll find my own guiding light.

Mourning in Moonlight

In the shadows of the night, I sit alone,
Beneath the moon's soft, silver tone.
I speak to the moon, in mourning's light,
Wondering how it still shines so bright.

"How do you glow?" I ask, full of woe,
In the loneliest hours when feelings grow?
Night descends, the silence deep,
My heart, in sorrow, starts to weep.
I strive to stay in rooms ablaze,
Pretend it's day, in myriad ways.
But darkness creeps, it starts to seep,
And thoughts once ignored, begin to creep.

The loudest cry, inside my soul,
You're gone, and that has taken its toll.
I mourn for you, again and again,
And for the life I lost, in endless pain.
Your absence casts a heavy weight,

A burden that alters fate.
It veers my dreams off course, it seems,
And shatters all my hopeful schemes.

I do not blame you, it's not your part,
Yet grief has woven into my heart.
It's hard to navigate this strife,
To live a fractured, wounded life.
So, moon above, I question thee,
How do you rise when the sun does flee?
For I am lost, unsure, in dread,
If I shall rise from mourning's bed.

In mourning's moonlight, dark and deep,
I find my soul, in silence, weep.
Yet maybe, like the moon so high,
I'll find a way to touch the sky.
To rise again, from sorrow's plight,
Embracing hope, in mourning's night.
For in the darkest hours, I might see,
A glimmer of what's left for me.

Honoring Your Last Breath

I'm sitting in silence, the pain begins to creep,
Knowing your last breath, a wound that seeps.
Every day haunted by our laughter's ghost,
Echoes in my ears, a melancholy boast.

Your smile, a vision when my eyes close tight,
In the realm of dreams, a bittersweet light.
I miss you more with each passing day,
Aching for your presence, yearning to say.

No breath shall I take for granted henceforth,
In the honor of you, a vow I take, an oath.
I'll carry your essence in all that I pursue,
A tribute in every step, in all that I do.

Your memory, a compass guiding my way,
Through the maze of life, in night and day.
Though you're gone, your spirit will stay,
In the breaths I take, in each new day.

JOURNAL
ENTRY

3

ECHOES OF LOVE

In the twilight of uncertainty, I stand before you, a humble architect of dreams, armed only with the fervent desire to paint our destinies in the hues of love. If only you could glimpse into the realm I envision, where our connection ignites a wildfire, a passionate blaze that sweeps through the world, leaving nothing untouched.

Our flames, fueled by the intensity of our connection, would consume the ordinary and mundane, turning the canvas of existence into a masterpiece of shared emotion. With you, I believe we could set ablaze the barriers that confine us, and together, we'd watch as our love engulfs the world in its transformative glow.

Yet, my love, it would not be a journey without its challenges. Like the undulating waves that caress the shores, our path would undeniably be marked by the ebb and flow of life's complexities. The journey of love, I propose, is not a placid pond but an expansive ocean, vast and deep. It promises moments of serenity, where the waters gently kiss the edges of our souls, and also tempests that demand resilience and courage.

A sanctuary where vulnerability is not a weakness but a strength. It is in the shared laughter and the silent support during trying times that the true essence of love reveals itself. It will be an adventure, filled with laughter that echoes in the canyons of our shared joy and with challenges that test the mettle of our connection. Yes, it will be hard—love, in its purest form, is not without its tribulations.

So, I ask you, seize this chance with me. Let us embark on this journey of love, where the flames of passion illuminate the darkest corners of our existence, and the soothing whispers of the ocean guide us through the challenging seas. Together, we can weather the storms, revel in the calms, and sculpt a narrative of love that transcends the ordinary—a story written in the language of our connected hearts.

Love Me, A Puzzle of Complexities

To love me, you must piece me together,
A puzzle without a picture, a mystery untethered.
Constantly misunderstood, I dwell in the unseen,
In layers of complexities, I am caught in between.

For humans, too, are intricate and deep,
Each heart and soul, their secrets to keep.
But for me, you must connect these threads,
To fully love me, unravel what's unsaid.

I am more than what meets the eye,
A string of feelings that reach for the sky.
Don't judge too quickly, don't rush to conclude,
In the depths of my being, true love is pursued.

With patience and care, you'll find the way,
To comprehend my essence, night and day.
For love's truest form is the one that sees,
The beauty within, past the surface, past degrees.

So, piece me together, embrace the unknown,
In the layers of my being, love shall be sown.
For in understanding, our hearts will unite,
And love will illuminate even the darkest night.

If You're Reading This...

From the day we met, you became my tomorrow,
A dream standing close, now a distant star to
    follow.
Your voice imprinted on my heart's quiet wall,
No other soul heard, your echo standing tall.

Come to me, let these words be a binding spell,
The only power I possess, a plea to make you
    well.
I spoke to the moon about you, whispered to
    stars above,
Asked the sun to shine, paint your world with
    love.

A beautiful day, an endless sky so blue,
Wished upon elements, each one for only you.
Told the rain to stay, keep sorrows far away,
But it chose to cleanse, make everything new,
    they say.

If you're reading this, know it's all about you,
In these lines, my feelings are raw and true.
The moon, the stars, the sun, and the rain,
Conspiring to bring you back, to end my silent
    pain.

Destined Encounters

Upon the screen, a vision strange,
A smile that made my heart rearrange,
Caramel skin like a canvas rare,
You held a gaze beyond compare.
In that moment's unknown and wondrous grace,
I felt destiny's warm embrace,
Hopes and dreams began to bloom,
As I gazed upon your light-filled room.

I wished upon a starlit night,
For fate to guide our paths just right,
To bring us close, our spirits meet,
And share a love so pure, so sweet.
The day arrived, our worlds entwined,
Your smile met mine, a treasure to find,
In person now, our souls aligned,
A journey started, hearts combined.

Attempts to stay connected strong,

But life's twists and turns went wrong,
Yet still, we had encounters bright,
Moments of joy, a shared sunlight.
Amid the positives, a storm did brew,
A negative encounter shook me true,
You saw a side, raw and unrefined,
A moment that played on my troubled mind.

Yet onward, still, I see your grace,
In every smile upon your face,
And when you turn your eyes to me,
I hope my light shines bright and free.
For though we've journeyed through the strange
        storm,
A light still guides, a love still warm,
In your glory, you still shine,
And I hope in my heart, you'll find the sign.
That amidst the trials we have faced,
There's still a chance for love's embrace,
In your gaze, I'll find my way,
And in your heart, forever stay.

I Longed for You

I longed for it to be you, yet my heart takes my
  hand,
Begging to release the notion of us, to understand.
My heart implores my mind repeatedly, you're
  not lost,
For she cradles you eternally, no matter the cost.

Through her vessels, you reside, coursing
  endlessly,
Touching every fiber of my being, always and
  freely.
Though I yearn for you, my heart insists, it's time
  to part,
Accepting that in letting go, you'll forever dwell
  in her tender art.

Chances of Forever

Take a chance, embrace the plea,
In mirrored depths, reflections free.
A beauty inside, an outer grace,
Two souls entwined, an intimate space.
See in my eyes the promise I make,
A union of hearts, an enduring stake.
Catering to wants, desires combined,
You and I, a harmony defined.

Like flowers bask 'neath sunlit gleam,
Like ocean waters in crystalline dream.
Our smiles unite, a radiant blend,
Outshining the sun, no shadows to send.
Even the rain, it glistens, envious gaze,
For our love's aura, a constant blaze.

On gloomy days, our sun aglow,
Together we shine, this vibrant tableau.
Amidst life's ebb, its rhythm and flow,

Together we stride, through highs and low.
Take a chance on this tranquil shore,
Our bond a fortress, forevermore.

Reciprocity

In the whispers of my heart, a burden lies,
A love unreturned, it's my own demise.
I dream of fate and cosmic ties that bind,
But in reality, it's just a trick of the mind.

Why did I choose this painful, twisted art?
To love you endlessly, and be torn apart.
Is this agony a product of my own creation?
A self-inflicted wound, a cruel damnation.

I crave your touch, your love so divine,
Lost in fantasies, in dreams I pine.
Do you, too, dream of us, of what could be?
Or am I alone in this desolate sea?

Trapped in a prison of my own design,
Longing for a love that will never be mine.
I yearn for you, with every beat of my heart,
Hoping one day, our love will find its start.

But until that moment, I'll remain confined,
In the hell of loving you, in the depths of my
	mind.
Perhaps, one day, you'll feel this love too,
And we'll break free together, me and you.

L.O.V.E

I've found a bittersweet truth,
A choice that binds my heart, yet often leads to
    ruth.
For love's a delicate dance, a balance we must
    seek,
A ribbon of joy and pain, where tears may stain
    our cheek.

I never knew that love could hurt, a lesson learned
    in time,
As I navigate this winding path, where emotions
    often rhyme.
A choice to give, to cherish, and to hold another's
    soul,
Yet with it comes the ache and doubt, the
    moments taking their toll.

Life's grandest dilemma, it seems, is love in all its
    grace,

For it's the force that drives us forward, a nev-
er-ending race.
But in these moments of despair, when love
becomes a thorn,
We find the strength to carry on, for in love, we
are reborn.

So let us live on valued energy, in love's embrace
we'll stay,
For though it can bring hurt and pain, it lights
our darkest day.
Life's greatest paradox, it's true, love's the essence
of our being,
And in the end, it's worth the pain, for love is
life, all-seeing.

JOURNAL ENTRY

HARMONY OF DREAMS

In the vast expanse between my dreams and reality lies a discordant symphony, where the notes of my aspirations clash with the harsh realities of my existence. It's a composition fraught with out-of-tune instruments—a cacophony of failures and wrong choices that seem to plague my every endeavor. Just when I believe I've found the right melody, a new challenge emerges, throwing my carefully crafted harmony into disarray.

My dreams, once vivid and promising, now feel distant, like melodies I can only hear others play. In the darkness of uncertainty, I find myself rendered silent, paralyzed by the fear of hitting the wrong notes, of stumbling through life without purpose or direction.

To be lost is to dwell in the shadows of the past, unable to make sense of its complexities, while simultaneously gazing into a future devoid of clarity or certainty. It's a state of absence, of standing on the precipice of one's own identity, unsure of where to turn or how to move forward.

In this moment of panic, with failure clawing at the door of opportunity and doubt whispering its seductive reassurances, I am gripped by paralysis. It feels as though I teeter on the edge of a chasm, staring into the abyss of irretrievable failure.

Yet, amidst the chaos and uncertainty, a profound lesson begins to emerge. Failure, once viewed as a foe to be vanquished, reveals itself as a steadfast companion, a friend that accompanies me through the highest of highs and lowest of lows. It is a constant presence, woven into the fabric of every endeavor, and every aspiration. And so, I have made a decision—neither to hate nor to love failure, but to simply acknowledge its presence and embrace the fear it incites.

For in the crucible of failure lies the opportunity for growth, for self-discovery, and for the transformation of discord into harmony. And so, I resolve to raise my voice above the clamor of doubt, to scream into the void, and hit the wrong notes if need be. For it is in the act of embracing failure and facing it head-on with courage and resilience that true progress is made, and the symphony of my life begins to find its rhythm once more. Only then can the harmony of my dreams be heard.

Where My Heart Stands

With pen in hand, I glimpse my heart's array,
In its quiet depths, emotions hold sway,
A beacon of hope, future's canvas unfurled,
Brighter days beckon, a painting of the world.
Seeking not fleeting happiness, transient and fast,
But a deeper solace, a peace that will last,
Contentment's embrace, like a tranquil stream,
In this quietude, my spirit finds its dream.

End goal resplendent, not just in sight,
But in every moment, every choice that's right,
A journey cosmic, woven by unseen hands,
A purpose gifted, by divine's grand plans.
In God's design, I find my destined place,
Guided by grace, a voyage to embrace,
So as I sit with pen, thoughts like stars above,
I write my story, woven with hope and love.

Whispers of Hope

Beneath the canvas of the endless night,
I cast my dreams with all my heart's delight,
Three shooting stars in the heavens' grand ballet,
I made my wishes, let me now convey.
First, upon a star, my voice did rise,
To wish for love to light your searching eyes,
Not just a glimpse, but see me, soul and skin,
My beauty, worth the love that's deep within.

The second star, I wished for pure success,
A life of peace, where my dreams find sweet
    caress,
To tread a path where spirit's light does gleam,
To be free, whole, in life's majestic stream.

Then, the third wish, a blend of love and grace,
For in their union, a peaceful life takes place,
A life where love and success combine,
To make my world, with joy and purpose, shine.
So here beneath the starry, cosmic sea,

I've woven wishes, bound eternally,
For love, success, and peace to beautifully align,
In life's grand mosaic, forever shine.

From Heartache to Growth

My mending heart embarked on a quest anew,
Chasing lives uncharted, a path to renew,
Adventures beckoned, growth on the horizon's
    gleam,
A fresh chapter unfurling, like an untamed
    dream.
No common threads of youth did I embrace,
Off to college's realm, a hopeful space,
Friendships to forge, connections to sow,
Yet echoes of voids past refused to let go.

Amidst the swirl of novelty and new,
My view remained obscured, a skewed avenue,
For every step I took, a shadow cast,
A reminder of the obstacles from the past.
Perhaps it was never meant to be,
These experiences I sought, a distant plea,
Yet once again, I tried to conform,
Molding my essence for acceptance's warmth.

But the friendship born from forced design,
Unleashed repercussions far from benign,
Beneath my stature, beneath my grace,
I found myself in a sorrowful place.
Disgusted with echoes of a version not me,
I longed to escape, to be truly free,
Fleeing my reflection, I fled from within,
Summer arrived, a chance to begin again.

A new view emerged, a change in the air,
A fresh perspective, a life to repair,
In the warmth of the sun, I sensed the shift,
But it was autumn's arrival that marked the uplift.
Through seasons and changes, a journey untold,
From heartache's grip to a spirit bold,
The past may linger, but transformation's begun,
For in each new chapter, a chance to outrun.

The winds of growth whisper a profound tale,
From struggles and pain, a strength is found,
In this unfolding story, through trials I remained,
A journey of healing, a soul unchained.

Pain's Poetic Journey

In shadows deep, where anguish lies,
A haunting echo, pain's disguise.
It lingers, searing, with icy touch,
A cruel companion, it hurts so much.
It starts within, an ache unseen,
A weight upon the soul, so keen.
Through shattered dreams and broken ties,
Pain's tears fall from weary eyes.

Like thunderstorms on a gloomy night,
It strikes the heart with all its might.
A disturbance wild, it leaves its mark,
A battle waged amidst obscurity.
Yet in this pain, a flame burns vivid,
A glimmer of hope within the strife.
For pain, though harsh, reveals the way,
To strength and growth, come what may.

It teaches lessons, deep and wise,

Unveiling truths beneath disguise.
The wounded heart, a vessel rare,
Transforms through pain into love's affair.
So let us not dismiss this pain,
But embrace it, dance in its rain.
For in its depths, we find our strength,
And rise above, to a greater length.

And when the storm has ceased to roar,
When pain's sharp edges hurt no more.
We'll bear the scars, a testament true,
To resilience, and the love we knew.
For pain, though fierce, can never break,
The spirit strong, the soul's awake.
And through the darkness, we'll ascend,
Embracing life, pain's story penned.

Love's Redemption

On this odyssey of growth, I tread,
Seeking love to mend, to lift my head,
Hoping love's touch will mend despair,
A longing deep, a soul laid bare.
Finally, someone glimpses the real me,
Validation dawns, the vision set free,
My first love's embrace, a salvation so pure,
Molding me, breaking chains, an open door.

Never before have I truly known,
Love's embrace, its warmth brightly shone,
A void within, an expanding space,
Seeking love's joy to fill, to erase.
Validation sought in love's tender grace,
Not for deeds performed, but a heartfelt embrace,
Chosen for being, not just for what's done,
A love that echoes beauty, inside and under the
    sun.

Love, the savior, the beacon in night,

Guiding me through darkness, igniting the light,
With pen in hand, these verses take flight,
For love's sweet essence is the source of my might.
In love's gentle touch, redemption I find,
A journey unwrapped, a soul redefined,
With every beat of the heart, the story begins,
Love's melody plays, where healing begins.

Journey Within

I stand with work ahead, a path untrodden,
Gathering hopes and fears, dreams and façade,
To break from chains, bad habits' grip,
Reclaim my spirit, let my true self slip.

Through nights of dreams and nightmares wild,
I journey deep, seeking to reconcile,
Strength to sever hindrance's grasp,
Listening to the whisper, the soul's gentle rasp.

Still in pursuit, seeking truth's embrace,
But now, in the right spaces, I find my place,
Casting aside futile shadows, I soar,
Letting my spirit guide me evermore.

Caring for others, a trait so true,
But self-love emerges, a hue anew,
For as I rise, I realize the key,
To truly love them, I must love me.

Shadows to Stars

In shadows deep, a battle's fought,
Where strength is tested, lessons taught.
Darkness, friend and foe combined,
Reveals the truths we've left behind.
A crucible where souls collide,
In ebony depths, we can't hide.
For in this void, a power dwells,
A tale of light the darkness tells.
Without the night, no day would break,
No gleaming dawn, no morning's wake.

Embracing dark, we face our fears,
And through its trials, our light appears.
Yet darkness wields a mighty sway,
Its hungry maw can lead astray.
Consuming fragments of our soul,
Until we lose sight of the whole.
But from this trial, strength is born,
As night gives way to hopeful morn.

A radiant orb, a cosmic fire,
A ball of light, soaring higher.
Enraptured stars, with envy's gleam,
Behold a soul, a radiant beam.
The moon, a witness, understands,
It longs to guide, with gentle hands.
As dawn ascends, the sun takes flight,
Banishing shadows, birthing sight.

For in the darkness, truths align,
A journey to the light's design.
So let the darkness shape your way,
For in its depths, you'll find the sway.
To rise, transform, and brightly burn,
A testament to lessons learned.

JOURNAL ENTRY

5

Liberation in Authenticity

In the realm of vulnerability, I grapple with a
     profound truth,
A revelation that beckons from the depths where
     the soul is found.
It's the courage to be disliked, a notion so divine,
For in the see-through cage, I've felt the weight
     of every judging eye.

Trapped within this transparent prison, where
     spectacles unfold,
As if the world's eyes upon me, a story to be told.
Nerve-racking, suffocating, the gaze that feels
     unkind,
A relentless scrutiny, a cage that confines.

Even those unknown, their gaze a silent storm,
An audience to my existence, a display to perform.
The fear of a misstep, a mistake profound,

Locked in this see-through cage, where judgment
knows no bound.
Yet, in this stifling atmosphere, where approval
is the air,
I've wielded a knife to my soul, sculpting a ver-
sion fair.

An idealized self, crafted to please,
Yet, in the shadows, I'm engulfed by unease.
The need for love, the hunger for approval,
They drive me to extremes, a constant loop, a
duel.
The sculpted self, a facade so grand,
Leaves me yearning, unhappy, in pain that won't
disband.
It feels like impending death, a specter always
near,
The weight of the cage, the gaze I live in fear.
But in the darkness, a glimmer of hope I perceive,
A lifeline extended by those who genuinely
believe.

So, I seek out the ones who will help me breathe,
Amidst the suffocating judgment, they offer a
    reprieve.
In their acceptance, I find solace, a sanctuary,
Breaking free from the cage, embracing
    authenticity.
For in the courage to be disliked, I unearth a key,
To liberate my soul, to let my spirit roam free.
No longer confined by the need for approval's
    embrace,
I breathe anew, guided by those who love, not
    just view.

Me

Deep in my soul, a girl unknown,
Hidden beneath layers, a self I disowned.
Unseen by the world, yet a glimpse they've
  caught,
Moments with her, but her essence, still sought.
A silent awakening through sessions with my
  pen,
A journey within, where she's finding her yen.

In new relationships, in actions, she's found,
Creating boundaries, a self, more profound.
In the mirror's reflection, a revelation came,
No real version reflected, just shadows and
  shame.
Envy for those who met her in moments untold,
The me I buried deep, a story to be told.

Apologies whispered for the pain I caused,
To the girl inside, for the scars that were paused.
In future moments, where mistakes may abide,

I beg forgiveness for the tears she may hide.
To her, I say, when you finally arrive,
Sorry for the suffering, for the tears that may
    thrive.

In the mirror once, our eyes did meet,
A glimpse of the real me, oh, what a feat.
To the me I am now, I express my remorse,
For not seeking you, in this turbulent course.
As I mourn the past, I thank you, dear friend,
For being what you could in my absence, attend.

I await the day when we finally unite,
Me, myself, and I, a reunion so bright.
To the girl within, with a voice to reclaim,
I can't wait to meet us and embrace our name.

Silent Symphony

Loneliness, a silent ache, misunderstood,
It's not the absence of a crowd, that's not the root.
Not the lack of faces or voices near,
It's the feeling that no one truly holds you dear.
In a room full of souls, still, you're adrift,
Lost in the sea of faces, your spirit shift.
No one notices, or perhaps, they don't dare,
To reach out, to listen, to truly care.

But in the depths of solitude's embrace,
I found a friend, a familiar face.
In the quiet moments, I came to see,
I have myself, and that's enough for me.
The hardest lesson life has taught,
Is to be your own, when love is sought.
So, in the shadows, I'll stand strong and true,
A friend to myself, when no one else knew.

Veiled Fragments

In my world the sun shines too bright,
I'm drained, holding on with all my might.
Fake smiles and laughter, an end in sight,
In this labyrinth, truth lost in the light.
Draped in cheerful colors, I wander lost,
A charade that exacts an unbearable cost.
Oh, how I yearn, the mask I toss,
Yet the fear of breaking down is a menacing
    ghost.

From me to you, I bear this weight,
Hoping someone might penetrate,
The facade I put up, anticipate,
The coming storm before it's too late.
Yet guilt plagues my weary mind,
To burden others, so unkind,
A battle within, chasing the wind,
An escape, oh how I wish to find.

I long to live, yet not like this,

Caught in a void of the abyss.
Prejudice shadow me in the midst,
Endlessly seeking love's sweet kiss.
Reflections I cast, in mirrors around,
Of who they want, I'm enduringly bound.
Tired of this echo, the only sound,
Within myself, I yearn to be found.

My Unspoken Song

In the shadowed corridors of regret I tread,
Mourning the life I yearned to have led.
A chance, a risk, I dared not embrace,
Trapped in the echoes of another's grace.
Yearning for a love not my own,
I sculpted myself in a mold overthrown.

Craving approval, a slave to their decree,
I lost the essence of what it meant to be me.
Alone, I stand with fractured pieces untold,
Shattered fragments of a story once bold.
In the tears that cascade down my face,
I glimpse the funeral for the mask, the misplaced.

I weep for the persona I wore for you,
Now, in solitude, tears unveil the true.
In the mourning of self, a requiem's plea,
To resurrect the one I was meant to be.
In the cemetery of echoes, I lay to rest,
The puppet I became, the role I suppressed.

A casket closed on conformity's decree,
I bury her deep, in the soul's tapestry.
A headstone stands, a solemn decree,
A reminder of the person I used to be.
Yet, from this grief, a phoenix may rise,
A rebirth of self, beneath the mourning skies.

Myself

I am the hidden, the girl deep inside,
Unveiling through words, where emotions confide.
In the dance of my pain, a silent rebirth,
Discovering the self, beyond the surface of earth.
In relationships new, I find my own way,
Crafting boundaries, creating the day.
Actions speak louder, a language of truth,
I am emerging, a self that's brand-new.

In the mirror's reflection, a truth unfurls,
No real version mirrored in the world.
Envy for those who glimpsed my concealed light,
The me I buried, now ready to fight.

I apologize to the girl within,
For the pain caused by the mask I've been.
In future moments where shadows may cast,
Forgive me for the tears that may last.

To myself, the past echoes in mourn,
Yet, gratitude whispers for lessons borne.
In absence, I thank the I that was,
For being a guide through the tumultuous buzz.

Awaiting the day when I fully see,
The me, the myself, and the I in harmony.
To the girl within, with a voice to reclaim,
I can't wait to embrace our shared name.

My Voice Echoes a Foreign Language

In echoes of my unheard cries,
A language lost, where understanding dies.
Explaining, screaming, words unfold,
Yet, in the silence, stories untold.

Misunderstood in every plea,
A dance of words, elusive and free.
I scream, I share, but still unseen,
In the quiet, perhaps, truth convenes.
In this room of silence, a language rare,
Where understanding whispers without a care.
I pause, I wait, will you perceive?
The unsung verses, these tales I weave.

Is My Reflection Me

Standing in the mirror, I shattered the frame,
Letting voices of judgments, dissolve into the
    same.
Lost in the fragments, where identity was sewn,
Terrified to return to a version not my own.
In the maze of self, I navigate the strife,
A war within, to unearth the authentic life.
Shattered illusions, like shards on the ground,
I seek the whispers of truth, yet to be found.
No longer confined by the images they drew,
I embark on a journey to rediscover what is true.
In the battlefield of self, courage takes the lead,
A war I must conquer, fueled by the seeds.
The canvas of existence, blank and unbound,
Painted with hues of self, a depth profound.
To win this war from within, I strive,
To unveil the essence, in which I truly thrive.

I've Said Too Much

In the cost of oversharing, I confess,
I got too comfortable, in my candidness.
Revealed parts of me, both near and dear,
Without realizing, in your presence, so clear.
I didn't intend to burden or make you care,
Just yearned to release what's inside, my truth
    laid bare.
Screaming to escape, to break free from doubt,
You were close, and my words spilled out.
In this moment, we both find our grace,
A connection formed through honesty's warm
    space.
For though I may have overshared, it's true,
I'm grateful you were here to listen, too.

I

Through the core of my essence, a saga unfurls,
A symphony of growth, a tale of the bold.
Me, once hidden, and I, the relentless seeker,
Myself, the sculptor, the future's blissful speaker.
Through the dance of my pain, my voice
        resonates,
Crafting futures, where hope navigates.
In actions and relationships, I define,
Myself liberated, a self that's genuinely mine.

The mirror reflects a revelation so bright,
No longer an imitation, but a radiant light.
No envy for those who met the concealed me,
For the self I buried is now unshackled, truly free.
No more apologies for the pain I caused,
The girl within, no longer paused.
In future moments, where scars may persist,
Forgiveness thrives, and tears desist.

To the past and present, gratitude expressed,

For guiding me through life's intricate quest.
In absence, I thank the versions of me,
For paving the way to the present I see.
Today, the trinity aligns with grace,
Me, I, and Myself, a harmonious race.
To the girl within, her voice reclaimed,
We walk hand in hand toward a life untamed.

Dreams come true in this bright future's glow,
As Me, Myself, and I together grow.
Thank you, past and present, for bringing me
     here,
To a life of fulfillment, where dreams appear.

JOURNAL ENTRY

6

ECHOES OF SALVATION

In the shadowed realms of my existence, I experienced a demise last night—a death that transcended the mere cessation of breath, a departure not marked by the stillness of the body, but by the fading embers of my spirit. It wasn't a physical demise but a spiritual unraveling that left me trembling, frightened for the remnants of my soul, for what is a soul without the resilient pulse of its spirit?

As the night unfolded, I navigated the labyrinth of trials—the trials that life, like an indifferent sculptor, carved into the very core of my being. Each trial, a chisel struck the marble of my essence, shaping and reshaping until the contours of my spirit were rendered unrecognizable. The pain inflicted, not by physical wounds but by the weight of burdens too heavy for the soul to bear.

In the depths of that spiritual abyss, I grappled with the notion of self—the self that once danced with dreams and sang with hope. Now, it lay shattered, fragmented like shards of glass, reflecting the harsh realities of a world that seemed indifferent to the fragility of the human spirit.

The trials became a tempest, a relentless storm that sought to extinguish the flame within me. I felt my spirit slipping away, like a whisper carried off by the wind, leaving behind a hollow echo of what once was. The darkness pressed in, and I feared that I had become a mere specter, a ghost haunting the corridors of my own existence.

Scared for my soul, I pondered the essence of life without the vivacity of spirit. For what is a soul without the spirited dance of its dreams and without the resilience that breathes life into every heartbeat? It seemed as though the very fabric of my soul was unraveling, the threads of vitality slipping through my trembling fingers.

Yet, as dawn approached, I found myself standing on the precipice of rebirth. The night of the spirit's demise had cleared the way for a new understanding—a revelation that even in the face of trials and pain, the spirit could be resurrected. The scars remained, etched into the tapestry of my soul, but they became a testament to the strength that emerged from the crucible of suffering.

In the wake of that spiritual death, I discovered a flicker of resilience, a spark that refused to be extinguished. The narrative of my spirit's demise became a prologue to a story of renewal, a testament to the capacity of the soul to rise from the ashes, reborn and unyielding in the face of life's relentless trials.

Submerged Serenity

I stand at the edge, where the sea meets the land,
Entranced by the beauty, so perfect and grand.
I dip my toe in the water, a cautious start,
Yet the cold stings, warning, a gentle heart.
Undeterred, I step forth, my foot in the sea,
A dance with the waves, a melody, wild and free.

Deeper I go, until submerged, lost in delight,
Unaware of the dangers that lurk out of sight.
Underwater, I stay, my breath as my guide,
In this blissful oblivion, where shadows reside.
Yet a voice breaks the silence, a cautionary word,
"Don't get greedy, the ocean is not what it seems
        to be."

The beauty deceives, hides perils beneath,
The waves, though enchanting, can bring about
        grief.
Fragile, we are, like the smallest of ripples,

In the ocean of life, where danger cripples.
As cuts and bruises may cover our skin,
So too can the choices that we make within.

The allure of perfection, a tempting hold,
Can lead us astray, in the vast, boundless fold.
Only as long as your breath allows, stay
    submerged,
But when you can't hold any longer, be urged.
To resurface, to find relief in the light,
Where the cycle of life restarts, breathe again.

The Unconditional We

Bound by the threads of love, I bid farewell,
To the pain of lost love, a tale to tell.
For my love knows no bounds, it shall prevail,
A beacon in darkness, a flower in bloom's trail.
In the midst of clouds, I am the guiding sun,
Shattering doubts, my light cannot be undone.
Through laughter, I create a joyful ton,
To banish your tears and make spirits run.

When life's burdens consume, I offer my shoulder,
A safe space to lean on, as emotions smolder.
I hold your crown, when grace has been
    disordered,
Guiding you back, as you find your way forward.

There's everything to love, in flaws be true,
They capture your heart, like drops of morning
    dew.
For I am love's embodiment, shining through,

In my own dark days, I need love from you.
Remind me of the love that you bestow,
A poem of affection, let these feelings grow.
With every word, let our love's essence flow,
In the arras of love, our spirits glow.

The Whispers of My Woes

In the silence of the night, I hear them stir,
The whispers of my woes, a haunting murmur.
Beneath the moon's soft, silver embrace,
My troubles awaken, finding their space.
Through the shadows, they begin to weave,
A tale of heartache that refuses to leave.
In the stillness, a symphony of sorrow,
Each whispered word, a bleak tomorrow.

I feel the weight of dreams unmet,
A heavy sigh, a deep regret.
The wind, a messenger of my despair,
Carries my woes through the midnight air.
The leaves rustle with a mournful sound,
As the echoes of my pain abound.
A spectral choir in the moonlit night,
Singing the verses of my silent plight.
Love lost, promises shattered in the dark,
The whispers tell a tale, leaving a mark.

In the chambers of my weary soul,
The whispers take their heavy toll.

Yet, within the darkness, a glimmer appears,
A spark of hope, calming my fears.
For in the whispers, a strength is found,
A resilient spirit, unyielding and profound.
So I let the night embrace my pain,
Allow the whispers, like gentle rain.
With each sigh, a healing starts,
A journey through shadows, mending hearts.
In the quiet hours, when the world's at rest,
I embrace the whispers, feeling blessed.
For within the echoes of my silent woes,
A resilient spirit within me grows.

God's Whisper

Fear not, my weary angel, for I am by your side,
In the darkest of times, in the depths of the night.
You shine so bright, a beacon of light,
To guide you through storms, I'll hold you tight.

The trials of this world may graze your soul,
But I've given you strength, and I've made you
    whole.
Your smile, like angel wings, will shield your
    heart,
A coat of armor, a work of art.

Imagine, my dear one, those wings unfurled,
A divine protection in a chaotic world.
With grace and courage, you'll carry on,
For in your spirit, my love is drawn.

Don't falter, my angel, be steadfast and strong,
In your journey on earth, where you belong.
I sent you here with purpose and grace,

To spread love and kindness in this earthly place.

So, my child, remember my words so true,
I'm with you always, watching over you.
In the face of darkness, let your light shine,
For everything will be alright, you are divine.

EPILOGUE

Thank You

I watch, as you navigate the storms I've penned,
Through my love lost and regrets, where shadows
    blend.
With each turned page, a bridge between our
    souls,
A silent connection, as my story unfolds.

As my pages get thinner, your presence grows
    near,
A love blossoming within, now vivid and sincere.
I long to offer more than words on this page,

Yet your touch, cherished reader, transcends the
    cage.

In the symphony of feelings, a dance of ink and
    tears,
I find myself falling, dispelling my fears.
For you, my reader, have become the art,
Leaving an eternal imprint on the canvas of my
    heart.

ABOUT THE AUTHOR

Kae unveils a profound artistic journey with her debut poetry collection, *The Whispers of My Woes*. Hailing from the realm of academia, Kae channels her passion for psychology into the realm of poetic expression, creating a poignant dialogue between her academic pursuits and the profound landscape of human emotion.

For Kae, writing transcends the boundaries of mere literary creation; it serves as an intimate and therapeutic dialogue with her own struggles and triumphs. In the quiet moments between academia and self-discovery, she finds solace in the timeless union of pen and paper, transforming the written word into a sanctuary of self-exploration. *The Whispers of My Woes* emerges as the result of this profound relationship—a collection of poetic writings that intricately weaves the threads of personal experience into the rich tapestry of the human condition.

Within the pages of her work, readers are invited to embark on a journey through the labyrinth of emotions, each verse a delicate brush stroke that paints the raw and authentic hues of life's challenges and triumphs. Kae's poetry is a mirror reflecting the shared struggles, joys, and complexities that define the collective human experience.

As a budding voice in the literary landscape, Kae invites readers to partake in her exploration of the universal language of emotion. Through the lyrical cadence of her words, she opens a window into the heart, inviting readers to find resonance in their own stories. *The Whispers of My Woes* is not just a collection of poetry; it is a testament to the transformative power of self-expression and the enduring strength found in the embrace of one's own narrative.

Kae's poetic journey is a testament to the resilience of the human spirit, and her work stands as an invitation to join her in the exploration of the profound beauty that emerges from the whispers of our collective woes.